Want 3 more books for FREE?

As a special thank you for downloading this book we would like to give you
3 MORE books absolutely FREE!

Scroll to end of this book to find out how!

A Smart Kids Guide To
SUPER SCOTLAND
A World Of Learning At Your Fingertips

By: Liam Saxon

INTRODUCTION – WHERE IS SCOTLAND?

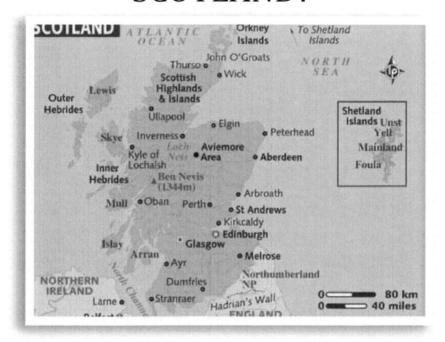

Scotland is located in the northern part of the United Kingdom, which includes Scotland, England, Wales and the northern most portion of Ireland. Scotland covers about one third of the United Kingdom's total landmass. Located off the western coast of continental Europe in the Atlantic Ocean, Scotland is still a European Country. Scotland actually has two names; the Gaelic name for Scotland is Alba.

WHAT IS THE SCOTTISH LANDSCAPE LIKE?

Scotland is made up of three major regions: the upper lowlands, the central lowlands, and the highlands and islands. The upper lowlands are just north of the United Kingdom and Scotland border, and most of the area is agricultural with rolling green hills and lush vegetation. The central lowlands are the most urban, populated and industrial of the three regions. Two major cities, Glasgow and Edinburgh, are located in the central lowlands. The highlands and islands are the largest of the three regions covering about fifty percent of Scotland's landmass. Dramatic and breathtaking scenery like deep lochs (or lakes), windy islands, and towering mountain peaks make up the area.

HOW MANY ISLANDS DOES SCOTLAND HAVE AND WHAT ARE THEY LIKE?

Scotland has nearly eight hundred total islands but man only populates 130 of them. The islands each have their own unique attributes and offer diverse wildlife and rich, lush landscapes. Rugged mountains found on the islands of Orkney or Shetland, and bird sanctuaries like the one found on the Isle of May, are just a few examples of the amazing natural discoveries to be made while exploring the Scottish islands.

WHAT IS THE CAPITAL OF SCOTLAND?

The city of Edinburgh is the capital of Scotland but you'll be surprised to learn that it is not also the biggest city. Glasgow is bigger than Edinburgh in terms of population. Scotland only has six officially recognized cities. These are Dundee, Glasgow, Iverness, Stirling, Aberdeen and of course, Edinburgh. Edinburgh has been the capital of Scotland since at least the 15th century. The most popular and well-known site in Edinburgh is the Edinburgh Castle.

WHAT IS THE EDINBURGH CASTLE?

The Edinburgh Castle is a massive fortress that dominates the breathtaking skyline of Scotland's capital city. The rock on which the castle is built has been occupied since as early at the Iron Age! That means people have been living on that mountain for over three thousand years! Edinburgh Castle was built right into the rock on the giant mountain, but we are not exactly sure when the site was built. Today the castle is both a tourist attraction and a historical conservation site.

TELL ME ABOUT OTHER SCOTTISH CASTLES

Scotland is definitely known for its many castles; in fact, did you know there are over three thousand castles in this small country? Some of these castles are actually some of the oldest known castles in Europe! Because the country spent so many years at war there was a need for strongholds and buildings to protect the people – therefore, many fortresses, or castles, were built over hundreds of years. Some are built high up on hills, like Edinburgh, while others are built with the ocean waves pounding in around it. People come from all over the world each year just to visit some of Scotland's castles.

WHAT LANGUAGES ARE SPOKEN IN SCOTLAND?

The Scottish people primarily speak English although Scottish English does not sound anything like British or American English. The native Scottish language, Gaelic Scottish, is only spoken by 1.5% of the entire population! The Scottish English is so different from English spoken elsewhere that sometimes foreigners have a hard time understanding it. For example, if you wanted to say, "You better just go easy," or "don't overdo it," in Scottish English you would say, "You'd better just caw canny."

TELL ME A LITTLE BIT ABOUT THE PEOPLE OF SCOTLAND

Many people think of red hair when they think of Scotland, and rightly so considering Scotland has a higher percentage – eleven percent – of red haired residents than anywhere else in the world! However, this is a far cry from everyone having red hair as the stereotypes suggest. In fact, you may be surprised to learn that the Scottish people have a heritage that originated in many other parts of the world! The native people to Scotland were actually called Picts, which translates to painted people, because of the ways in which they used to paint their bodies.

WHAT IS THE WEATHER LIKE IN SCOTLAND?

Because so much water surrounds Scotland, since it is in the Atlantic Ocean, the weather will often change quite drastically, making it hard to predict. And, with so many different regions, the weather is different across the country. But one type of weather that you can depend on in Scotland is rain! Out of 365 days in the year, it will rain about 250 of them somewhere in Scotland! Otherwise the climate is temperate and the country experiences all four seasons.

WHAT TYPES OF FOOD DO THE SCOTTISH TYPICALLY EAT?

The Scottish people have a varied diet but are known for quite a few unique dishes. One of their most popular dishes is fish and chips, which is fried white fish, like Haddock, served with french fries or chips. Shortbread is another dish the Scots are famous for. Shortbread is a buttery biscuit or cookie and can be found in different varieties all across the country. Sometimes shortbread comes dipped in chocolate or with a jellied fruit filling. A famous Scottish drink is the Irn-Bru, which is a carbonated, fruit drink, like a fruit flavored soda.

WHAT IS A TRADITIONAL SCOTTISH MEAL?

A meal called Haggis is probably the most well known of all traditional Scottish meals. Haggis is also the country's national dish! Haggis is made from a sheep – but not the sheep's meat! Rather it is made up of what is called the sheep's pluck, which means the sheep's heart, lungs and liver. These juicy bits are cooked with minced onion, oatmeal, suet, spices and salt and then mixed into a soup stock. Traditionally cooks would simmer the stew in the stomach of the sheep although now it is often cooked in big pots. Would you try it?

WHO ARE SOME FAMOUS PEOPLE FROM SCOTLAND?

There are a few world known authors that hailed from Scotland including Sir Walter Scott and Robert Louis Stevenson, author of A Child's Garden of Verses. The famous inventor, Alexander Graham Bell, who invented the telephone, also came from Scotland. Musicians Rod Stewart, Annie Lennox and Jimmy Shand are Scotland natives too, as are actors Sean Connery and Robbie Coltrane!

WHAT ARE SOME FAMOUS SCOTTISH MYTHOLOGIES?

Scotland is filled with rich stories and strong mythologies that have been passed down for ages. Some famous Scottish myths include the Loch Ness Monster, the gift of Second Sight, and the Stone of Destiny. The Stone of Destiny is also called the Stone of Scone and it is a long block of redstone that was used to coronate the kings and queens of Scotland. The gift of Second Sight is the belief that someone can see into the future! The Scottish myths also tell rich tales of fairies, goblins, sprites, and elves.

TELL ME ABOUT THE LOCH NESS MONSTER

The word loch means lake, and Loch Ness Monster is simply put, a lake monster. In the stories the Loch Ness lives in the lakes of the Scottish Highlands. Some people believe that the idea of the Loch Ness came from an actual animal that descended from the plesiosaur, an ancient dinosaur. However, despite this theory, modern scientists don't believe that the Loch Ness is real and they call it a modern-day myth. The stories of the Loch Ness Monster are so popular that some people have nicknamed the monster Nessie.

WHAT KINDS OF ANIMALS ARE FOUND IN SCOTLAND?

Because Scotland's landscape is so varied, so is its wildlife. The Scottish Highlands are known for having the highland cattle and red deer, which are both native to Scotland. You'll also find the golden eagle, red kite, red squirrel and wildcat in Scotland. Ocean animals include whales, dolphins, seals and even puffins!

DID THE UNICORN COME FROM SCOTLAND?

The unicorn, a mythical creature to some and a real creature to others, is actually Scotland's official National Animal! Unicorns are meant to represent beauty, youth, innocence and pride and are thought to bring joy and have healing powers. unicorns are found in fiction stories all over the world but many Scottish people believe they existed at one point and are now extinct. What do you believe?

WHAT ARE BAGPIPES?

Bagpipes are a popular, Scottish musical instrument. The instrument consists of reed pipes that are attached to a bag. The player holds the bag in his arms and squeezes it while blowing into a mouthpiece, and in this way, music comes out of the reed pipes. The instrument is quite loud but fun to hear played. It is an old Scottish instrument and often played during ceremonies, like weddings, or during traditional festivals, or ceilidhs. The instrument is associated with Scotland but it's also played in France and Ireland.

WHAT ARE KILTS?

Kilts actually look just like skirts that are typically worn by women, but in Scotland, men typically wear the kilts. The kilts are knee-length and pleated, made of tartan cloth, which is a fabric with criss-crossing colors and lines, looking very close to plaid. Originally tartan was made by weaving bits of wool together, although now it is made from a variety of materials. The kilt used to be worn every day by the Highlanders though now it is just used for special purposes, like ceremonies and festivals.

WHAT IS HIGHLAND CULTURE?

Highland Culture is sometimes called Gaelic Culture and refers to the rich culture of the Scottish people from the Highlands. The highlands landscape was so rugged that the people who lived there were originally divided into clans and each clan was ruled by a chief. In fact, the kilt was developed during this clan time because they needed clothing that allowed them to climb over the rugged hills comfortably. The Highlanders were said to be always ready for battle so traditions of strength came from their lifestyle. Some of these games include the hammer toss and the caber toss, which is a long, heavy pole.

WHAT IS CEILIDH?

The people of Scotland often talk about a ceilidh,
especially you visit the Scottish Highlands. But what
exactly is a ceilidh? A ceilidh is a traditional Gaelic social
gathering like a festival or party, usually held in a town's
hall or hotel. During the gathering traditional folk music is
played while participants dance. Ceilidh's used to also be a
time for telling stories and acting out tales for
entertainment and songs were often sung. Today people
still have Ceilidhs and they are fun way to do something
traditionally Scottish.

Claim Your 3 FREE Books!

Thank you for reading this book - we truly appreciate your interest, reviews and feedback! It gives us the motivation to keep publishing new books that inspire and educate people around the world!

As a special thank you, we would like to give you 3 Free Books!

Here's how to claim yours:

1) Leave a review on this book - We love hearing your kind words!
2) Once you have left your review, get your free books here:

>> http://ebookrebel.com/3freebooks <<

Made in the USA
San Bernardino, CA
12 October 2016